# the Rainbow

D. A. Yang-Omand

TRILOGY CHRISTIAN
PUBLISHERS

*Tustin, CA*

Trilogy Christian Publishers
A Wholly Owned Subsidiary of Trinity Broadcasting Network
2442 Michelle Drive
Tustin, CA 92780

*Love Under the Rainbow*

Copyright © 2024 by D. A. Yang-Omand

All rights reserved, including the right to reproduce this book or portions thereof in any form whatsoever.

For information, address Trilogy Christian Publishing

Rights Department, 2442 Michelle Drive, Tustin, Ca 92780.

Trilogy Christian Publishing/ TBN and colophon are trademarks of Trinity Broadcasting Network.

For information about special discounts for bulk purchases, please contact Trilogy Christian Publishing.

Trilogy Disclaimer: The views and content expressed in this book are those of the author and may not necessarily reflect the views and doctrine of Trilogy Christian Publishing or the Trinity Broadcasting Network.

10 9 8 7 6 5 4 3 2 1

Library of Congress Cataloging-in-Publication Data is available.

ISBN 979-8-89333-117-2

ISBN 979-8-8933-118-9 (ebook)

# Contents

Letter 1 .................................................1

Letter 2 .................................................5

Letter 3................................................. 8

Letter 4 ...............................................11

Letter 5 ............................................... 14

Letter 6 ............................................... 18

Letter 7................................................ 24

Letter 8 ............................................... 28

Letter 9 ............................................... 32

Note ................................................... 35

# LETTER 1

Dear child of mine,

You will never know how much love I hold for you. We are going through such a rough time right now. I believe fake love would be to put on a happy face, tell you all the things you wanted to hear, and then make judgment behind your back. Fake love would be to hide my true feelings and my moral beliefs while telling you it's okay to do things I don't agree with. These adversities are breaking my heart, this bridge between us. Do you know how I long to have a relationship with you? Look at all the things that we respected in each other, all the life moments we shared with one another! To me, real love is to respect who we both are, for us to forget forceful or manipulative actions and be whole with one another. When someone says you must approve of everything they do or they will not have a relationship with you, it feels manipulative. I can love all of you and show you love where you are. I can leave the things I don't agree with in God's hands. We can view the things we like about each other, all the beautiful and wonderful things, and truly love one another, although we may have different viewpoints. Relationships are hard, but love is worth it. I fear all sins, not just sexual sin, but the ones I'm struggling with right now. We all experience this. I pray that I can be changed daily and that I can do a better job of dying to myself and picking up my cross every day. Romans 6:23 says, "Fear of the Lord, for the wages of sin is death, but the gift of God is eternal life in Christ Jesus our Lord." I said the part above as a whole; not all people have sexual sin, but all people have sinned. We are born into it. Child of mine, I truly love you.

Dear Lord,

Please have me be one with Jesus and help me hold on to Him, the true vine. Holy Spirit, teach and lead us both. I will always love You, Lord. In Jesus Christ, I pray, amen.

**Romans 6:23 (NIV)**

*For the wages of sin is death,*

*but the gift of God is eternal life*

*in Christ Jesus our Lord.*

LETTER 2

Dear child of mine,

Do you know we all fall short of the glory of God? When you look at us, your parents, you see two broken people trying to make a life together. There are things we didn't share with you because we felt those things should be kept private. You may have viewed one of us as pushy and overbearing, not understanding that they were experiencing a cheating spouse. Everyone's story is different. Other people in the LGBTQ community may have been abused by their parents. Some dads make bonding time with their daughters based solely on male-based activity. Other times, parents hurt their children sexually. Some parents hurt their kids with words; some hurt their kids by withholding time or resources. Some hurt by having too many or too few responsibilities, not balancing out life. The list goes on and on. If I could, I would give the LGBTQ community a big hug. You are a survivor. You are fearfully and wonderfully made. Child of mine, I truly love you.

Dear Lord,

Thank You that I am so fearfully and wonderfully made. Please help me see myself and others as You do, Lord. Please help me to overcome all fear, doubt, and confusion over me and my parents' life. Thank You for Your love and mercy! Thank You for loving me so. In Christ's name, amen.

### Psalm 139:13-16 (NIV)

*For you created my inmost being;*

*you knit me together in my mother's womb.*

*I praise you because I am fearfully and wonderfully made;*

*your works are wonderful, I know that full well.*

*My frame was not hidden from you when I was made in the secret place,*

*when I was woven together in the depths of the earth.*

# LETTER 3

Dear child of mine,

You don't need to change anything. You are perfect the way you are made. Once you seek His will and walk in His ways, you will feel the unending love of Jesus Christ and know who you are with Him! We're born by God's own hands, and I know He loves you. You may feel like you are confused, or you may feel you're not confused. You may feel no one understands you. You may feel you have no identity without the LGBTQ community, but I say you do. Dwelling in God's community, you are and will feel loved, and you will find joy. I'm not saying all churches or people of God do a good job with this, but in this bigger picture, you are loved! In Christ, you have everything you ever needed! First, love

God with all of your heart, then love yourself. When you love yourself, you have a more gratifying love to give to others. Ask the Holy Spirit to guide you and comfort you with all things that you do. There are things God knows about you that you don't even know about yourself. Child of mine, I truly love you!

Father God,

You are holy and good. Father, open my eyes to the world around me. Help me to see the things as you do. Help me to love and be kind, this I know for the Word tells me so. If I could give You one thing today, it would be to help someone on the way. Thank You for Your love and care; this is what I have to share. Father, I love You! Forever, Your child!

## Psalm 139:17-18 (KJV)

*How precious also are thy thoughts unto me,*

*O God! How great is the sum of them!*

*If I should count them, they are more in number than the sand;*

*When I awake, I'm still with thee.*

## LETTER 4

Dear child of mine,

I ask of you to pray and ask our Father to close deceiving doors and spirits. Ask the Holy Spirit to bring healing to everyone that has ever felt pain in their identity and their sexuality. May the Holy Spirit lead us and guide us in all His love and truth. There are so many people that hurt in the world for so many reasons. Romans 13:8 instructs us to owe no one anything, except the debt to love one another, for he who loves another has fulfilled the law.

Dear Lord,

You are holy and good. I honor You, Father. Open my eyes and the eyes of the world around me, too. Help me see things as You do. Help me to love and be kind. If I could give You one thing today, it's to help someone on the way. Thank You for Your love and care. This is what I have to share. I love you, Father. Forever, Your child.

**Romans 13:8 (NIV)**

*Let no debt remain outstanding,*

*except the continuing debt to love one another,*

*for whoever loves others has fulfilled the law.*

# LETTER 5

Dear child of mine,

Every person has the right to make choices for themselves and to make choices for their children. There is a lot of cruelty in this world today. Some people from the church community are cruel. There's cruelty from the LGBTQ community. Cruelty resides in politics and in entertainment. We are made to love, my child. John 13:34 (ESV) says, "A new commandment I give to you, is that you love another just as I have loved you, you are to love one another."

> *Show proper respect to everyone, love the family of believers, fear God, honor the emperor.*
>
> 1 Peter 2:17 (NIV)

I wish we all could just learn to honor others and to be kind to them. With that, we would have so much pain eased. There is a place to be honest about our deep beliefs, and there is a place to say, "This is where we are," and honor what we have. Do you agree with every person? Can we live in peace and harmony? I believe we can if we wish to do so. We can show love and respect to our parents, families, friends, and colleagues, even if we have different points of view. If we say to ourselves, *I don't know their full story; I don't truly know all their ins and outs*, judgment may not be so quick to fall on our minds. I have seen one pick a partner based off shared weaknesses, and more often than not, those are the bonds we are traumatized by. Dear child of mine, you are loved.

Dear Father,

I honor You because You are holy and without fault. You are all-knowing! Your ways are higher than mine. Lord, please forgive me for the times I have judged anyone. Help me see things as You see them. Thank You for Your love. In Christ, I pray. Amen.

## John 13:34 (NIV)

*A new command I give you:*

*Love one another.*

*As I have loved you,*

*so you must love one another.*

## LETTER 6

Dear child of mine,

In my eyes, the world, at large, has been caught up in greed and dishonesty, curse words, self-reasoning, and sins of many kinds. All these things have hurt our souls.

> Now the works of the flesh are evident, which are adultery, fornication, uncleanness, lewdness, adultery, sorcery, hatred, contentions, jealousies, outburst of wrath, selfish ambitions, dissensions, hearsays, envy, murders, drunkenness, revelries, and the like; of which I tell you beforehand, just as I also told you in time past, that those who practice such things will not inherit the Kingdom of God. But the fruit of the Spirit is love, joy, peace,

*long-suffering, kindness, goodness, faithfulness, gentleness, self-control. Against such there is no law. And those who are Christ's have crucified the flesh with its passions and desires. If we live in the Spirit, let us walk also walk in the Spirit. Let us not become conceited, provoking one another, envying one another.*
Galatians 5:19-26 (NKJV)

The Bible says that when we commit a sexual sin, we sin against our own body. This sin hurts us the most because of the chemical and emotional attachments we may feel while committing the sin. When you have sex, you release dopamine. Some people seek out more and more sex as a dopamine fix, resulting in sexual addiction. God intended for us to multiply and replenish the earth.

God intended for man and woman to bond, have intimacy, and to have pleasure. A great relationship can bring growth and healing neurochemicals, like healthy releases of oxytocin and dopamine. Most people want to be loved and have a person that they can share the closest, most intimate parts of themselves with. We all want to be loved, to work together, to build a life, to feel safe and secure. Lots of people have been sad, confused, and lonely and just want to reach out to another human being in general. Our loneliness allows us to be blinded. You are not alone! My child, you truly are loved!

> *Do not remember the sins of my youth, nor my transgressions; According to Your mercy remember me, for Your goodness' sake, O Lord.*
>
> Psalms 25:7 (NKJV)

*Flee from sexual immorality. All other sins a person commits are outside the body, but whoever sins sexually, sins against their own body.*

1 Corinthians 6:18 (NIV)

Unfortunately, some of us had our first sexual experiences as victims of an abuser; others had a choice. These things may have shaped us in ways we repeated in our adult lives. This can be a very painful scar for some of us. Some people go on to be abusers; others live in shame that isn't theirs to carry and become victims. Few are blessed and become victors! Some people are abused in their adult lives, and this is where sin started. I have seen many women turn to other women after abusive relationships with men. I don't have a lot of statistics, but I have seen this from friendships over the past years. Many people are broken and want to find a safe harbor for their souls. Child of mine, you are loved and safe with Our Father!

Dear God,

You are good, and Your ways are peace and love! Jesus, healer of the broken, please heal me and all those who hurt me in any way. Holy Spirit, please lead and guide me in all truth. In Christ, I pray. Amen.

## Psalms 25:7 (NIV)

*Do not remember the sins of my youth*

*and my rebellious ways;*

*according to your love remember me,*

*for you, LORD, are good.*

## LETTER 7

Dear child of mine,

We as people live in a body, we have a soul, and we are a spirit. Released pleasure receptors are often repeated seeing how we enjoy the experience behind them. There are things that connect with those receptors that are good and some bad. If one cheats on you, it hurts your soul and your emotional health. It hurts your mentality, and it hurts your spirituality too, as the pain dwells within your soul it can become detrimental. Sin of all kinds hurt our souls. When we commit a sin, we become one with it, until we ask for forgiveness. We should especially treat our bodies with great respect even when it comes to the choice of committing sexual sins.

*Therefore, if anyone is in Christ, he is a new creation; old things have passed away; behold, all things have become new. Now all things are of God, who has reconciled us to Himself through Jesus Christ, and has given us the ministry of reconciliation, that is, that God was in Christ reconciling the world to Himself, not imputing their trespasses to them, and has committed to us the word of reconciliation. Now then, we are ambassadors for Christ, as though God were pleading through us: we implore you on Christ's behalf, be reconciled to God.*

2 Corinthians 5:17-20 (NIV)

You are loved.

Dear Lord,

Thank You for Your great love. Thank You for being holy where we have failed. Thank You for the grace You give to break all unhealthy soul ties in all sins of our youth. I thank You! Thank You for Your willingness to forgive all those sins and failures of mine, yesterday's and today's. Help me be more like You every day! My hand is outreached for You. So, Father, take my hand and lead me. God, in stillness, may I find Your voice. Thank You for loving me. In Christ, I pray. Amen.

## 1 Corinthians 6:19 (ESV)

*Or do you not know that your body*

*is a temple of the Holy Spirit within you,*

*whom you have from God?*

*You are not your own...*

## LETTER 8

Dear child of mine,

There are failures in your parents and failures in our belief systems. There are failures and things our eyes have seen and our hands have held. Your healing journey will be different than ours! Just as we all had different weaknesses and sins, we're all exposed to different things in life. But others in this world at some time in their life have been hurt by sin and have hurt others by their sin. Sin hurts, and all the world has had some of it at some time. I have hope for you wherever you may be on this journey. If you are scared and confused, I have hope for you. If you feel angry, I have hope for you. It is the church's job to tell you the truth in love. My child, please know, there are failures on all sides and sins of all kinds, people hating people, groups hating groups. Give yourself truth in love and lend a hand; so many people don't know how to do that. There are so many people that are cruel. There are those that want to be politically correct and allow opinions to take over one another. Ask every day for God to lead you by the Holy Spirit. I have always found the Book of Psalms to be healing and healthy to my soul, The Book of John a place to learn about Jesus, the Book of Acts a place to see how the Holy Spirit came and dwelled among us. I study the book of Ephesians because it's the gift of joy and family, and it's there for those of us that have had broken love. I have come face to face with Jesus. On our broken road, call out to the One with healing in His hands. You'll come face to face as well. Lean on Him because He is gentle. Lean on Him because He has come to give us life. Lean on Him because He can restore us, the broken.

Dear Lord,

Here I am, Abba; please lead and guide me into all truth. This world has no hold over me. Help me to heal, and guide me along this path. I will follow. Trusting You, I let go of yesterday. I thank You and receive Your blessings. In Christ, I pray. Amen.

### **Galatians 2:20 (NIV)**

*I have been crucified with Christ and I no longer live,*

*but Christ lives in me.*

*The life I now live in the body,*

*I live by faith in the Son of God,*

*who loved me and gave himself for me.*

## LETTER 9

Dear child of mine,

Let us be free from anything that is unfitting to God. He calls us to walk in love and to be holy. May our Lord, King of glory, free us of the sins of yesterday and help us walk in love and freedom.

- See Ephesians 5:1-7.
- See 1 Thessalonians 4:7.
- See Galatians 5:19-24.

Dear Father,

You are holy, and as a new person in Jesus, I am called to be holy. Please keep me and help me be found worthy through Your blood. Help me to be Your loving child all the days of my life. Please make my life path straight and help me to grow in the faith. Thank You, Father. In Jesus' name, amen.

## 2 Corinthians 5:17-21 (NIV)

*Therefore, if anyone is in Christ, the new creation has come: The old has gone, the new is here! All this is from God, who reconciled us to himself through Christ and gave us the ministry of reconciliation: that God was reconciling the world to himself in Christ, not counting people's sins against them. And he has committed to us the message of reconciliation. We are therefore Christ's ambassadors, as though God were making his appeal through us. We implore you on Christ's behalf: Be reconciled to God. God made him who had no sin to be sin for us, so that in him we might become the righteousness of God.*

This book has a collection of love letters written to the LGBTQIA+ community and their families. It's my hope and prayer that this book brings reconciliation. May it draw you closer to the Father, Son, and Holy Spirit. This is to be viewed as a healing word and journaling book. Blessings to you and your loved ones.

Author D. A. Yang-Omand,
Certified Christian Counselor

www.ingramcontent.com/pod-product-compliance
Lightning Source LLC
Chambersburg PA
CBHW070439230125
20719CB00004B/107